COUNTRIES OF THE WORLD

Sweden

by Shannon Anderson

BELLWETHER MEDIA • MINNEAPOLIS, MN

Blastoff! Readers are carefully developed by literacy experts to build reading stamina and move students toward fluency by combining standards-based content with developmentally appropriate text.

Level 1 provides the most support through repetition of high-frequency words, light text, predictable sentence patterns, and strong visual support.

Level 2 offers early readers a bit more challenge through varied sentences, increased text load, and text-supportive special features.

Level 3 advances early-fluent readers toward fluency through increased text load, less reliance on photos, advancing concepts, longer sentences, and more complex special features.

★ **Blastoff! Universe**

This edition first published in 2024 by Bellwether Media, Inc.

No part of this publication may be reproduced in whole or in part without written permission of the publisher. For information regarding permission, write to Bellwether Media, Inc., Attention: Permissions Department, 6012 Blue Circle Drive, Minnetonka, MN 55343.

Library of Congress Cataloging-in-Publication Data

Names: Anderson, Shannon, 1972- author.
Title: Sweden / by Shannon Anderson.
Description: Minneapolis, MN : Bellwether Media, Inc., 2024. | Series: Blastoff! Readers : countries of the world | Includes bibliographical references and index. | Audience: Ages 5-8 | Audience: Grades 2-3 | Summary: "Relevant images match informative text in this introduction to Sweden. Intended for students in kindergarten through third grade"– Provided by publisher.
Identifiers: LCCN 2023003562 (print) | LCCN 2023003563 (ebook) | ISBN 9798886874334 (library binding) | ISBN 9798886876215 (ebook)
Subjects: LCSH: Sweden–Juvenile literature.
Classification: LCC DL609 .A63 2024 (print) | LCC DL609 (ebook) | DDC 914.8504–dc23/eng/20230130
LC record available at https://lccn.loc.gov/2023003562
LC ebook record available at https://lccn.loc.gov/2023003563

Text copyright © 2024 by Bellwether Media, Inc. BLASTOFF! READERS and associated logos are trademarks and/or registered trademarks of Bellwether Media, Inc.

Editor: Rebecca Sabelko   Designer: Gabriel Hilger

Printed in the United States of America, North Mankato, MN.

Table of Contents

All About Sweden	4
Land and Animals	6
Life in Sweden	12
Sweden Facts	20
Glossary	22
To Learn More	23
Index	24

All About Sweden

Stockholm

Sweden is on a large **peninsula** in northern Europe. It is part of a group of countries called **Scandinavia**.

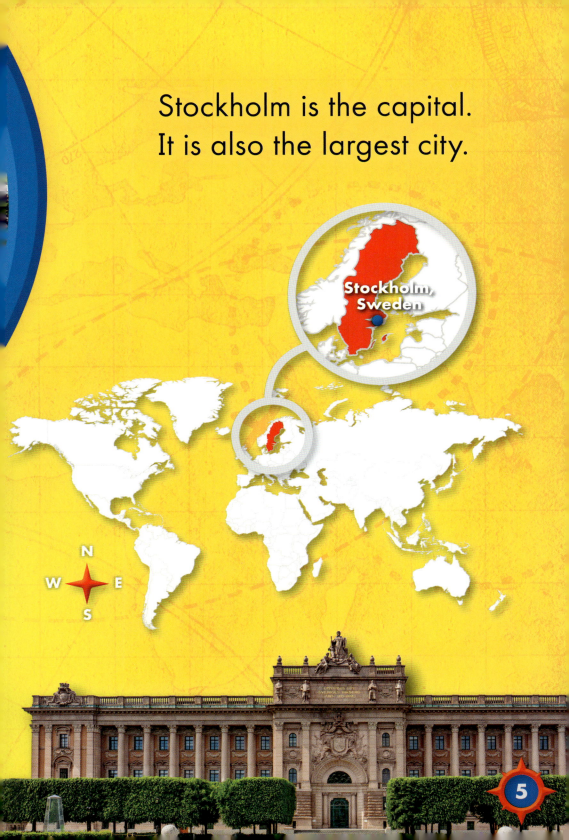
Stockholm is the capital. It is also the largest city.

Land and Animals

Forests cover much of Sweden. The north lies in the **Arctic Circle**.

Mountains line the west. Central Sweden has **plains** and lakes. Rocky islands are found off the coast.

Kebnekaise

Size: 6,880 feet (2,097 meters) tall
Famous For: the highest mountain in Sweden

Winters in the north
are long and very cold.

Winds from the Atlantic Ocean control the **climate** in the south. Winters are mild. Summers are warm.

Wolves hunt moose and deer in the country's thick forests.

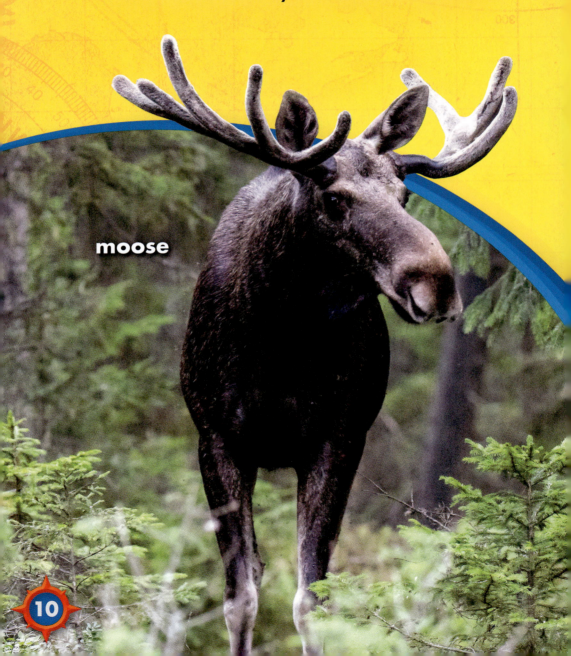

moose

Animals of Sweden

gray wolf

moose

common chaffinch

Atlantic herring

Songbirds sing at backyard feeders. Herring swim along the coasts.

Life in Sweden

People who live in Sweden are called Swedes. They speak Swedish.

Many people belong to the **Lutheran** Church of Sweden. Most people live in southern cities.

hiking

berry picking

Swedes enjoy being outdoors. They fish, hike, and pick berries.

Soccer is a top sport. People like skiing and ice fishing in winter.

ice fishing

Swedes enjoy Swedish meatballs and pickled herring. Parties have tables of food called *smörgåsbords*.

Swedish Foods

Swedish meatballs

pickled herring

smörgåsbords

kanelbullar

Fikas are daily breaks. They include coffee and a treat. Cinnamon buns, or *kanelbullar*, are common.

Midsummer

Midsummer welcomes summer. People dance around a **maypole**.

maypole

St. Lucia Day is December 13. Children carry candles down snowy streets. Swedes enjoy their **culture** all year!

Sweden Facts

Size:
173,860 square miles
(450,295 square kilometers)

Population:
10,483,647 (2022)

National Holiday:
National Day (June 6)

Main Language:
Swedish

Capital City:
Stockholm

Famous Face

Name: Greta Thunberg
Famous For: a teen climate activist who was TIME's 2019 Person of the Year

Religions

- other: 9%
- none: 33%
- Church of Sweden (Lutheran): 58%

Top Landmarks

Drottningholm Palace

Jukkasjärvi

Viking City of Birka

Glossary

Arctic Circle—an imaginary line that circles the top of the globe, parallel to the equator

climate—the usual weather conditions in a certain place

culture—a custom or belief of a certain group of people

Lutheran—relating to a type of Christianity that follows Martin Luther and his teachings; Christianity is a religion that follows the words of Jesus Christ.

maypole—a tall pole decorated with ribbons and flowers

peninsula—a section of land that extends out from a larger piece of land and is almost completely surrounded by water

plains—large areas of flat land

Scandinavia—a region of northern Europe that includes Sweden, Denmark, and Norway

To Learn More

AT THE LIBRARY

Albertson, Al. *Moose*. Minneapolis, Minn.: Bellwether Media, 2020.

Dean, Jessica. *Sweden*. Minneapolis, Minn.: Jump!, 2019.

Tucker, Zoë. *Greta and the Giants: Inspired by Greta Thunberg's Stand to Save the World*. London, U.K.: Frances Lincoln Children's Books, 2019.

ON THE WEB

Factsurfer.com gives you a safe, fun way to find more information.

1. Go to www.factsurfer.com.
2. Enter "Sweden" into the search box and click 🔍.
3. Select your book cover to see a list of related content.

Index

animals, 10, 11
Arctic Circle, 6
Atlantic Ocean, 9
capital (see Stockholm)
city, 5, 12
climate, 9
coast, 6, 11
Europe, 4
fishing, 14, 15
food, 16, 17
forests, 6, 10
hiking, 14
islands, 6
Kebnekaise, 7
lakes, 6
Lutheran Church of Sweden, 12
map, 5
Midsummer, 18
mountains, 6, 7
peninsula, 4
people, 12, 15, 18

picking berries, 14
plains, 6
say hello, 13
Scandinavia, 4
skiing, 15
soccer, 15
St. Lucia Day, 19
Stockholm, 4, 5
summer, 9, 18
Sweden facts, 20–21
Swedish, 12, 13
winter, 8, 9, 15

The images in this book are reproduced through the courtesy of: Oleksiy Mark, front cover; Kristyna Henkeova, front cover; Jens Ottoson, pp. 2-3, 14-15; Imfoto, p. 3; Mistervlad, pp. 4-5, 5; Nataliia Sokolovska, p. 6; Folio Images/ Alamy, pp. 6-7; BeyondImages, pp. 8-9; ricok, p. 9; ArtBBNV, pp. 10-11; AYImages, p. 11 (gray wolf); Martin Mecnarowski, p. 11 (moose); Hans Baath, p. 11 (common chaffinch); Duncan Noakes, p. 11 (Atlantic herring); trabantos, p. 12; Levranii, pp. 12-13; Tsuguliev, p. 14 (berry picking); Hemis/ Alamy, p. 15; norikko, p. 16 (Swedish meatballs); Svetlana Monyakova, p. 16 (pickled herring); Filip Jakovljevic, p. 16 (*smörgåsbords*); Bernd Juergens, p. 16 (*kanelbullar*); Maskot/ Getty Images, p. 17; Fotos593, pp. 18-19; titoOnz, p. 20 (flag); Michael Sohn/ AP Images, p. 20 (Greta Thunberg); Tommy Alven, p. 21 (Drottningholm Palace); Viktorishy, p. 21 (Jukkasjärvi); TT News Agency/ Alamy, p. 21 (Viking City of Birka); Piotr Krzeslak, pp. 22-23.